BASIC & IMPORTANT TERMS OF ECONOMICS

SHIVARAMAKRISHNA VADUGU

Made with ♥ on the Notion Press Platform
www.notionpress.com

Contents

Contents

Preface

From A to Z economics basic terms which are useful to the economics students. To get more effectiveness from this book. We collected terms but researching and finding meaning of that word leave it to the students. My suggestion is only three words per day is enough, if it feels easy than continue it to the more words. All these words are very necessary to economics students these words are repeats every time in their career. We hope this book helps as much as possible.

ONE
CHAPTER A

A

- Absolute advantage
- Adaptive expectations
- Adverse selection
- Advertising
- Agency costs
- Agricultural policy
- Agriculture
- Aid
- Amortization
- Animal spirits
- Antitrust
- Appreciation
- Arbitrage
- Assets
- Auctions
- Average

TWO

CHAPTER B

B

Backwardness
Balance of payments
Balanced budget
Bank
Bankruptcy
Barriers to entry and exit
Barter
Basel 1 and 2
Basis point
Bear
Behavioral economics
Beta
Big Mac index
Black economy
Black-Scholes
Bonds
Boom and bust
Bounded rationality
Brand
Bretton woods

Bubble
Budget
Bull
Business confidence
Business cycle
Buyer's market

THREE

CHAPTER C

C

- Cannibalise
- Capacity
- Capital
- Capital adequacy ratio
- Capital controls
- Capital flights
- Capital gains
- Capital intensive
- Capital markets
- Capital structure
- Capitalism
- Cartel
- Catch-up effect
- Central bank
- Charity
- Classical dichotomy
- Classical economics
- Closed economy
- Collateral
- Collusion

Command economy
Commoditization
Commodity
Common goods
Communism
Comparative advantage
Competition
Competitive advantage
Competitiveness
Complementary goods
Compound interest
Concentration
Conditionality
Consumer confidence
Consumer prices
Consumer surplus
Consumption
Contagion
Contestable market
Convergence
Corruption
Cost of capital
Cost-benefit analysis
Creative destruction
Credit
Credit creation
Credit crunch
Creditor
Crony capitalism
Crowding out
Currency board
Currency peg
Current account

FOUR
CHAPTER D

D

Deadweight cost and loss
Debt
Debt forgiveness
Debt-equity ratio
Default
Deficit
Deflation
Demand
Demand curve
Demographics
Deposit insurance
Depreciation
Depression
Deregulation
Derivatives
Devaluation
Developing countries
Development economics
Diminishing returns
Direct taxation

Discount rate
Discounted cash flow
Diseconomies of scale
Disequilibrium
Disinflation
Disintermediation
Diversification
Dividend
Division of labor
Dollarization
Dominant firm
Dumping

FIVE
CHAPTER E

E

Econometrics
Economic and monetary union
Economic indicator
Economic man
Economic rent
Economic sanctions
Economics
Economies of scale
Effective exchange rate
Efficiency wages
Efficient market hypothesis
Elasticity
Emerging markets
Endogenous
Engel's law
Enron
Enterprise
Entrepreneur
Environmental economics
Equilibrium

Equities
Equity
Equity risk premium
Eurodollar
Evolutionary economics
Excess returns
Exchange controls
Exchange rate
Exogenous
Expectations
Expected returns
Expenditure tax
Export credit
Exports
Externality

SIX

CHAPTER F

F

- Factor cost
- Factors of production
- Factory trade
- FDI (Foreign Direct Investments)
- Federal Reserve System
- Financial centre
- Financial instrument
- Financial intermediary
- Financial markets
- Financial system
- Fine tuning
- Firms
- First-mover advantage
- Fiscal drag
- Fiscal neutrality
- Fiscal policy
- Fixed costs
- Flotation
- Forecasting
- Foreign trade policy

SEVEN

CHAPTER G

G

- G7, G8, G10, G21, G22, G26
- Game theory
- GATT (General Agreement on Tariffs and Trade)
- GDP (Gross Domestic Product)
- Gearing
- General agreement on tariffs and trade
- General equilibrium
- Generational accounting
- Giffen goods
- Gilts
- Gini coefficient
- Global public goods
- Globalization
- GNI (Gross National Income)
- GNP (Gross National Product)
- Gold
- Gold standard
- Golden rule
- Government
- Government bonds

Government debt
Government expenditure
Government revenue
Growth

EIGHT

CHAPTER H

H

- Hard currency
- Hawala
- Hedge
- Hedge funds
- Herfindahl-Hirschman index
- Homo economics
- Horizontal equity
- Horizontal integration
- Hot money
- House prices
- Human capital
- HDI (Human Development Index)
- Hyper-inflation
- Hypothecation
- Hysteresis

NINE

CHAPTER I

I

Imperfect competition
Imports
Income
Income effect
Income tax
Incumbent advantage
Index numbers
Indexation
Indifference curve
Indirect taxation
Inelastic
Inequality
Inferior goods
Inflation
Inflation target
Information
Infrastructure
Innovation
Insider trading
Institutional economics

Institutional investors
Insurance
Intangible assets
Intellectual capital
Interest
Interest rate
International aid
IMF (International monetary fund)
ILO (International Labour Organisation)
International trade
Intervention
Investment
Invisible hand
Invisible trade
Inward investment

TEN

CHAPTER J

J

Job

ELEVEN

CHAPTER K

K

Kleptocracy

TWELVE

CHAPTER L

L

- Labour
- Labour intensive
- Labour market flexibility
- Labour theory of value
- Laffer curve
- Lagging indicators
- Laissez-faire
- Land
- Land tax
- Laws of economical activities
- Leverage
- Leveraged buy-out
- Liberal economics
- Liberalization
- Life
- Life-cycle hypothesis
- Liquidity
- Liquidity preference
- Liquidity trap
- Lock-in

Long run
Lump of labor fallacy
Lump-sum
Lump-sum tax
Luxuries

THIRTEEN
CHAPTER M

M

Macroeconomics
Manufacturing
Marginal
Market capitalization
Market failure
Market forces
Market power
Mean
Mean reversion
Median
Medium term
Menu costs
Mercantilism
Mergers and acquisitions
Microeconomics
Minimum wage
Misery index
Mixed economy
Mobility
Mode

Modeling
Modern portfolio theory
Monetarism
Monetary neutrality
Monetary policy
Money
Money illusion
Money markets
Money supply
Monopolistic competition
Monopoly
Monopsony
Moral hazard
Most-favored nation
Multiplier

FOURTEEN

CHAPTER N

N

National debt
National income
Nationalization
Natural monopoly
Natural rate of unemployment
Negative income tax
Neo-classical value
Network effect
Neutrality
New economy
New growth theory
New trade theory
NGO (Non government organization)
Nominal value
Non-price competition
Normal goods
Normative economics
NPV (Net Present Value)
Null hypothesis

FIFTEEN

CHAPTER O

O

Oligopoly
Open economy
Open-market operations
Opportunity cost
Optimal currency area
Optimum
Option
Output
Output gap
Outsourcing
Over the counter
Overheating
Overshooting

SIXTEEN

CHAPTER P

P

- Patents
- Path dependence
- Peak pricing
- Percentage point
- Percentile
- Perfect competition
- Population
- Positional goods
- Positive economics
- Poverty
- Poverty trap
- PPP (Purchasing Power Parity)
- Precaution
- Prediction
- Preference
- Present value
- Price
- Price discrimination
- Price regulation
- Price and earnings ratio

Prisoners dilemma
Private equity
Privatization
Probability
Producer prices
Producer surplus
Production function
Productivity
Profit
Profit margin
Profit maximization
Progressive taxation
Propensity
Property rights
Prospect theory
Protectionism
Public goods
Public spending
Public utility
Public – private

SEVENTEEN

CHAPTER Q

Q

- Quantity theory of money
- Quartile
- Queueing
- Quota

EIGHTEEN

CHAPTER R

R

- Random walk
- Rate of return
- Rate of return regulation
- Ratings
- Rational expectations
- Rationality
- Rationing
- Real balance effect
- Real exchange rate
- Real interest rate
- Real options theory
- Real terms
- Recession
- Reciprocity
- Redlining
- Reflation
- Regional policy
- Regression analysis
- Regressive tax
- Regulation

Regulatory arbitrage
Regulatory capture
Regulatory failure
Regulatory risk
Relative income hypothesis
Rent
Rent-seeking
Replacement rate
Repo
Repo rate
Required return
Rescheduling
Reservation wage
Reserve currency
Reserve ratio
Reserve requirements
Reserves
Residual risk
Restrictive practice
Returns
Revealed preference
Ricardian equivalence
Ricardo, David
Risk
Risk averse
Risk-free rate
Risk management
Risk neutral
Risk premium
Risk seeking

NINETEEN
CHAPTER S

S

Satisfaction
Savings
Say's law
Scalability
Scarcity
Scenario analysis
Secondary market
Securities
Securitization
Seignorage
Seller's market
Seniority
Sequencing
Services
Shadow price
Shareholder value
Shares
Sharpe ratio
Shock
Short-termism

Shorting
Signaling
Simple interest
Smith, Adam
Social benefits or costs
Social capital
Social market
Socialism
Soft currency
Soft dollars
Soft loan
Sovereign risk
Speculative motive
Spot price
Spread
Stabilization
Stability and growth pact
Stagflation
Stagnation
Stakeholders
Standard deviation
Standard error
Statistical significance
Sterilized intervention
Sticky prices
Stochastic process
Stocks
Stress-testing
Structural adjustment
Structural unemployment
Subsidy
Substitute goods
Substitute effect

Sunk costs
Supply
Supply curve
Supply-side policies
Sustainable growth
Swap
Systematic risk
Systemic risk

TWENTY

CHAPTER T

T

Tangible assets
Tariff
Tax arbitrage
Tax avoidance
Tax base
Tax burden
Tax competition
Tax efficient
Tax evasion
Tax haven
Tax incidence
Taxation
Technical progress
Terms of trade
Time series
Time value of money
Total return
Trade
Trade area
Trade cycle

Trade deficit and surplus
Trade unions
Trade-weighted exchange rate
Tragedy of the commons
Transaction costs
Transfer pricing
Transfers
Transition economies
Transmission mechanism
Transparency
Treasury bills
Trough
Trust

TWENTY-ONE

CHAPTER U

U

- Uncertainty
- Underground economy
- Unemployment
- Unemployment trap
- Unions
- Usury
- Utility

TWENTY-TWO

CHAPTER V

V

- Value added
- Value at risk
- Variable costs
- Velocity of circulation
- Venture capital
- Vertical equity
- Vertical integration
- Visible trade
- Volatility
- Voluntary unemployment

TWENTY-THREE

CHAPTER W

W

- Wage drift
- Wages
- Wealth effect
- Wealth tax
- Weightless economy
- Welfare
- Welfare economics
- Welfare to work
- Windfall gains
- Windfall profit
- Winner-takes-all markets
- Withholding tax
- World Bank
- WTO (World Trade Organization)

TWENTY-FOUR

CHAPTER X

X

TWENTY-FIVE

CHAPTER Y

Y

Yield

TWENTY-SIX

CHAPTER Z

Z

Zero-sum game

Thank You

Thanks to every reader. All the best for your future in economics and finance career.

Printed by Libri Plureos GmbH in Hamburg,
Germany

9 798890 023520